I0455100

# COMMON LAW, SOVEREIGNTY, RESTORING
the
## Tea Party Republic
Second Edition

**\* \* \***

## Answering 101 Questions
About the Common Law

Preserving Sovereignty

Restoring the Republic

## A. Nicholaw, PhD
Professor of Common Law

Copyright © 2012 A. Nicholaw, PhD

All rights reserved, including the right to reproduce this book
in any portion hereof in any form whatsoever,
without written permission of Andy Nicholaw, PhD.

ISBN: 1478321601
ISBN-13: 9781478321606

*IN MEMORIUM*
*To*
*Red Feather*

*Russell Edward Herrmann*
*American Indian*

1927–1994

# Table of Contents

# Preface

C ommon Law, Sovereignty, Restoring the Tea Party Republic consists of five basic parts in recognizing the importance our forefathers gave to the unity of our states in forming a United States of America. The nucleus of such unity was brought about after some twenty-two years of consideration after Benjamin Franklin, in 1755 said: "join or die."

Today, with the advent of communications, the truth is as dearly sought as then. No amount of suppression is the suppression of truth when communication is at its facile best. We are being kept in abject ignorance by our own government as the world explodes with information and knowledge to uplift all mankind with the grace of the rights of man.

This book is for today. It is divided into sections for ease of understanding.

Section One: *The Common Law.* Why it is also known as God's Law; Natural law; Organic Law. And where did it come from? Due to the current "tea party" movements resulting in a projected return to our Constitution and the restoring of our Republican form of government, renewed interest in the Common Law is upon us. Why?

Section Two: *Preserving Sovereignty.* What is sovereignty and have we lost it? Where does our government relate to sovereignty, or where does our state relate? How does sovereignty relate to the Common Law and to a Republican form of government granting representation to others for governance?

Section Three: ***The Tea Party Republic.*** What was it in 1773, and now? How do we restore our Republic when abuses of government have robbed us of our life, liberty, and pursuit of happiness? How do we successfully restore our Republic?

Section Four: ***How to Restore the Republic*** – A simple and practical solution emanating from the heart of a Republican form of government. Benjamin Franklin first warned we must unite, or die; Thomas Paine called out, the common man is supreme; Thomas Jefferson put the process in writing; and George Washington warned the people must defend always.

Section Five: **101 *Most Asked Questions*** with answers about the Common Law. Presents the Common Law and Truths to recognize.

Americans are in the dark about the Common Law; in the dark about their Sovereignty; and are only now beginning to restore the Tea Party Republic by claiming the right to life, liberty, and pursuit of happiness. The truth is uncovered by questioning. And that is what this book does: answers questions ***About the Common Law, Preserving your Sovereignty, Restoring our Republic.*** The answers need actions to take: Section Four and Section Five do that for you.

Section Four is a boilerplate ballot. Get it on a ballot in your State. Take a Tea Party Action!

Section Five will greatly assist all interested in specific questions concerning the Common Law.

With due respect and brotherhood,

— Author

# CAN YOU ANSWER THESE QUESTIONS?

## Questions: General

(Answer yes or no: true or false.)

1. Is America a Democracy?

2. Is the United States a central bank?

3. Can lawyers lawfully serve in the Congress?

4. Were there enough congressmen in Congress Assembled as the Federal Reserve Act passed?

5. It only takes a majority in Congress to pass a bill.

6. Was slavery outlawed before the Civil War?

7. Our Constitution is Supreme Law of the Land.

8. A Congressman, if desired, is empowered to vote for the "good of the country".

9. By Constitutional Procedure, Congressmen get paid when they are not in Congress Assembled.

10. Our Representatives read all legislation that they vote on.

# ANSWERS: General Questions

1. FALSE. America is a Republic.

2. FALSE. The "faith and credit" of the people is the central bank for the U.S.A.

3. FALSE. They hold "titles of nobility", and are excluded by the 13$^{th}$ Amendment.

4. No. Only two were present. Three are required. Congress was not assembled.

5. YES.

6. YES. Many served as free men under George Washington.

7. NO. The 9$^{th}$ & 10$^{th}$ Amendments reserved it.

8. NO. A Congressman is a representative. He can only vote for his constituents.

9. FALSE. The Sergeant of the House takes roll. No show, no pay.

10. NO. Our representatives have aides and others read the laws and advise. Unlawful.

# Introduction

The Tea Party of 1773 wasn't just the dumping of tea in Boston Harbor. It was the signal to the world that man was sovereign, had natural rights protected by laws in common, and that those rights were foremost amongst all nations. The local, Boston issue of taxation without representation only heightened the inalienable, organic rights of man.

The chronology leading to the Tea Party of 1773 did not just happen with a bunch of rogues deciding to rebel against the English oppressors in a spur of the moment. There were many abuses of power leading to the Boston Tea Party; however, it is most important to historically note that it was not the Americans who signaled the first rebellion. It was Pontiac, Chief of the Ottawa Indians. And Benjamin Franklin, in 1754 then published the "Join or Die" cartoon.

*The Pennsylvania Gazette* published this cartoon in 1754, urging the colonies to unite. With it was an article by Benjamin Franklin promoting his Albany Plan for a central colonial government. The plan marked a significant step toward unity.

Although the rough picture of a snake separated into eight pieces marked with the initials of New England, New York, New **Jersey**, Pennsylvania, Maryland, Virginia, North Carolina, and South Carolina, was first used in an attempt to unite the colonies as early as 1754 as the Albany Plan of Union, it was premature and not supported by the Colonists until revived by Pontiac's attack upon the British in May, 1763, and made a standard by the Tea Party patriots two years later when the British passed the Sugar Act and the Stamp Act, which allowed British soldiers to be quartered throughout the colonies.

**To show that the correct tax had been paid, British officials used stamps on goods sold in Britain and the United States.**

Alarmed, the Colonists prepared to unite as they struggled to peacefully remain a colony of English rule. It simply did not work. On May 10, 1773, England passed the Stamp Act claiming sovereignty over America, and resulting in Patrick Henry's famous resolutions: the fifth summed it all.

"Resolved, therefore, that the General Assembly of this Colony have the only and sole exclusive right and power to lay taxes upon the inhabitants of this Colony."

It was now clear: every attempt to vest such power in any...persons...other than the General Assembly would destroy British as well as American freedom. No taxation without representation. America would have to assert its exclusive rights.

Suddenly, with this speech, Patrick Henry became a spokesman for the common people, and the two parties: Patriots, or Whigs; and Loyalists – those who remained loyal to England – also called 'Tories", were born.

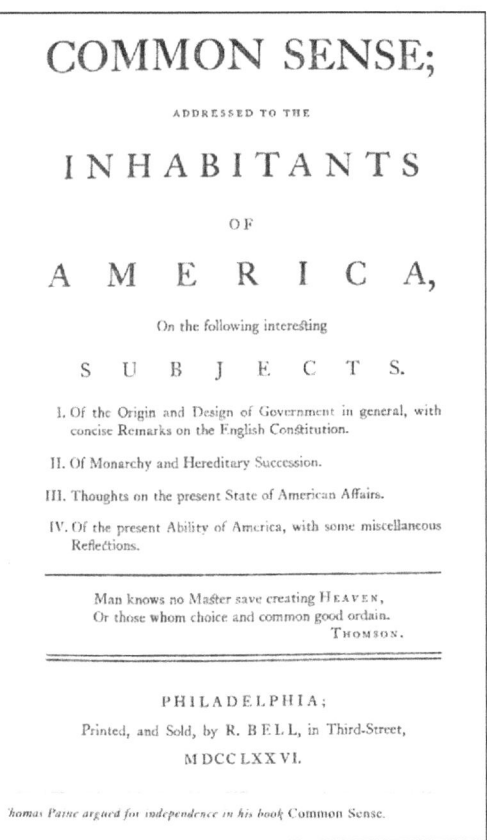

## COMMON SENSE;

ADDRESSED TO THE

### INHABITANTS

OF

### A M E R I C A,

On the following interesting

### S U B J E C T S.

I. Of the Origin and Design of Government in general, with concise Remarks on the English Constitution.

II. Of Monarchy and Hereditary Succession.

III. Thoughts on the present State of American Affairs.

IV. Of the present Ability of America, with some miscellaneous Reflections.

Man knows no Master save creating HEAVEN,
Or those whom choice and common good ordain.
THOMSON.

PHILADELPHIA;

Printed, and Sold, by R. BELL, in Third-Street,

MDCCLXXVI.

Thomas Paine argued for independence in his book Common Sense.

Henry's words became the general outcry for the Tea Party and was the beginning of the revolutionary movement in the American colonies.

The Patriots were the backbone of the Republic. The Boston Tea Party formulated between 1773 and 1776. Our country is that Nation uniting all of the colonies into one nation: the United States of America embracing a Republican form of government wherein man, the citizen, was to become the ultimate law of the land possessing original ordained rights.

The Boston Tea Party was known as the "Destruction of the Tea"; but when the Patriots, as Mohawk Indians marched into town, with axes and tomahawks on their shoulders, a fifer playing by their sides, within a few days, a Boston street ballad called: "The Rallying of the Tea Party" not only identified the two leaders—Warren and Revere—by name, but gave the Tea Party its origin and history in protecting common rights.

> "Rally Mohawks! Bring out your axes,
> And tell King George we'll pay no taxes
> On his foreign tea."
>
> ............................................................
>
> Our Warren's there, and bold Revere
> With hands to do and words to cheer
> For Liberty and laws."

It is no wonder, then, that this is the hallmark of liberty and freedom for every man as foreseen and upheld by our forefathers when creating the ninth and tenth Amendments to our Constitution.

"The enumeration In the Constitution of certain rights, shall not be construed to deny or disparage others retained by the people."

The people, again, were the ultimate beneficiary of all rights and powers within a Republican form of government. They were protecting their voice and guarding the limited powers to be relinquished to a federal government after granting it federal authority to govern, and to become a nation subservient to the desires and wishes of the sovereign states ultimately, represented by the people as: sovereign man.

"The powers not delegated to the United States by the Constitution, or prohibited by it to the States, are reserved to the States respectively, or to the people."

The Tea Party of yore is very much alive today. All over America the strong desires and morals which our founding fathers clearly laid down in 1776 return for all mankind to re-assert and claim once more.

"We hold these truths to be self-evident: that all men are created equal; that they are endowed by their creator with certain inalienable rights; that amount these are life, liberty, and the pursuit of happiness; that to secure these rights, governments are instituted among men, deriving their just powers from the consent of the governed; that whenever any form of government becomes destructive of these ends, it is the right of the people to alter or to abolish it, and to institute new government, laying its foundation on such principles, and organizing its powers in such form, as to them shall seem most likely to effect their safety and happiness."

The expression reverberated in the hearts and minds of all men then, and needs to be restored today. Its effect, as expressed by the concluding paragraph of the Declaration of Independence, is as much alive in meaning and intent for all mankind as when expressed in 1776. The Spirit of '76, which was so near exhaustion at Valley Forge, was kindled by such resolve.

"We, therefore, the Representatives of the United States of America, in General Congress Assembled, appealing to the Supreme Judge of the world for the rectitude of our intentions, do, in the Name, and by the Authority of the good People of these Colonies, solemnly publish and declare, that these United colonies are, and of Right ought to be Free and Independent States, that they are absolved from all allegiance to the British crown, and that all political connection between them and the State of Great Britain is and ought to be totally dissolved, and that as Free and Independent States they have full Power to levy War, conclude Peace, contract Alliances, establish Commerce, and to do all other Acts and Things, which Independent States may of right do – and for the support of this Declaration, with a firm reliance on the protection of divine Providence, we mutually pledge to each other our Lives, our Fortunes, and our sacred Honor."

## WE THE PEOPLE

"The wings of the Spirit
Fly low, low, low.
How else?

But to pick up
The Common Man
Who struggles endlessly,
In pursuit of fleeting Liberty
Once inalienably guaranteed
By loftier Constitutions
Cemented in the earth
Of natural Common Laws.

Rise, rise up, Oh Spirit.
The Common Man awakes.
Your Time has come again."

– A. Nicholaw

## DATES & EVENTS CHANGING HISTORY

1754 Benjamin Franklin urges Colonists to unite.

1765 Parliament passes Stamp Act, which taxes
Colonists on all printed items.

1770 The Boston Massacre on March 5. Five
Colonists are killed.

1773 The Boston Tea Party on December 16.

1774 The First Continental Congress meets in Philadelphia
in September.

1776 **Common Sense** by Thomas Paine sold 400,000 copies to
three million Colonists. Common Sense swept across the
world to introduce the Rights of Man & a Republic.

1776 The Second Continental Congress meets
in Philadelphia June 7; Thomas Jefferson submits
Declaration of Independence July 2
which is approved July 4 and is publicly read to all America
on July 8.

1781 President George Washington's Farewell
Address reminds all Americans how to
preserve the new Republic.

Section One

# THE COMMON LAW

# CAN YOU ANSWER THESE QUESTIONS?

## Questions: About the Common Law

(Answer yes or no: true or false.)

1. The Common Law is international, a part of every nation, of every culture.

2. Does the Common Law protect your Liberty?

3. Is Natural Law the same as ethical or moral law?

4. Can a money judgment be granted under the Common Law?

5. Is the Common Law a written law for man to follow?

6. Common Law establishes right from wrong.

7. The Common Laws are really a declaration of the guaranteed rights of man as being sovereign with free will granted by his creator.

8. The Common Laws grant us Life, Liberty, and the Pursuit of Happiness.

9. Do our Municipal Laws follow the guidelines of the Common Laws?

10. Are the Common Laws ultimately the Law of the Land?

## ANSWERS: Common Law

1. TRUE  The Common Law is based upon ancient records, traditions, and customs throughout all cultures.

2. YES  The Common Law is the grantor of sovereignty as it is based upon organic law & created a Constitution.

3. YES  It is the nature of things: all men are created equal.

4. NO  It only determines rights and wrongs. Money judgments are Equity, Statutory & Code Laws.

5. NO  It is an unwritten law added into the Republican form of government as a rule of decision.

6. TRUE  It cannot award damages, only injury or loss.

7. YES  Declarations are Natural Rights guaranteed as all men are created equal with the same sovereign rights.

8. TRUE  The Declaration of Independence clearly includes Common Laws as declared rights under God.

9. YES  They are the lowest of a vertical construction of laws under the State and the Union of States.

10. YES  We the people, in Article X, have reserved all rights not delegated or granted to the United States or to the States.

## Section One: THE COMMON LAW

The Common Law is the cornerstone of the Constitution *for* the United States of America. It is the "unwritten law" behind the balanced government which we so richly enjoy: The Executive, the Legislative, and the Judicial branches all forming a triangle: checking, balancing, and seeing that the other branch upholds the very Constitution which **We the People** ordained & established.

Yet, often we forget that all government comes from us, and that our Common Laws are simply expressed in what our forefathers said in delegating powers to a national government while they kept for themselves the whole of the nation and their express sovereignty. Thus they could not have revealed their intent in framing a Constitution more plainly. Could it be expressed any more simply?

> *"The nature & intention of a Constitution is to prevent governing by a party, by establishing a common that shall limit and control the power and impulse of party, and that says to all parties:*
>
> ## *"This far shall thou go and no farther."*

The "common", as established, is a set of Common Laws which remind the national government that they are not the Nation; that all powers were not delegated to them; and that there were definite limits for them to follow in pursuance of the Constitution. We secured for ourselves certain rights which are: Life, Liberty, and the Pursuit of Happiness. But to preserve these rights, the Common Laws had to be recognized and to become living rights for all citizens.

The Common Law, as frequently defined, is the unwritten law, including those principles, usages, and rules of action applicable to the government and security of persons and property which do not rest for their authority upon any express or positive statute or other written declaration, but upon statements of principles found in the decisions of the courts.

The Common Law is inseparably, therefore, identified with the decisions of the courts and can be determined only from such decisions in former cases bearing upon the subject under inquiry.

As distinguished from statutory or written law, it embraces that great body of unwritten law founded upon general custom, usage, or common consent, and based upon natural justice, of reason. It may otherwise be defined as custom long acquiesced in or sanctioned by immemorial usage and judicial decision. Hawaii's land laws are a perfect and unique example in that they are based on such ancient tradition, custom, practice, and usage.

The thirteen original states, in their constitutions and declarations of rights, recognized the Common Law as it had prevailed in the Colonies. And the rule of decision, should there be doubt or conflict with statutory or current, existing code law, remains with the Common Laws rendered prior and subsequently to the date of the statute.

Our Common Laws establish rights, especially concerning rights of property. Such rights extend even today – such as the right of inspection of corporate records by a shareholder, and a statute providing an analogous remedy. Such analogous remedy is merely cumulative to the Common Law remedy. The updated difference lies in recovery of damages. The Common Law remedy does not provide damages, only insuring an established right to due process and procedure of the laws in common in obtaining a remedy.

This, then, required the introduction of rules to be identified and followed. Such rules of the Common Laws, therefore, became protective in nature. Some of the most important are found in our Constitutional Amendments. The Fourth Amendment gives us the right to be secure in person, houses, papers, and effects against unreasonable searches and seizures; the Ninth Amendment encompasses all rules not found within the Constitution by specifically stating:

*"The enumeration in the Constitution of certain rights shall not be construed to deny or disparage others retained by the people."*

But of most singular importance, respecting the sovereignty of each and every one of us is our Seventh Amendment which ultimately expresses the people retain power over the executive, legislative, and judicial branches of the national government:

*"In Suits at common law, where the value in controversy shall exceed twenty dollars, the right of trial by jury shall be preserved, and no fact tried by a jury shall be otherwise re-examined in any Court of the United States, than according to the rules of the Common Law"*

The Common Law is the final Rule of Decision in any Court in any state of the United States of America, not because it is the Supreme Law of the Land, but because the supreme authority is the voice of **We the People** who control even the judiciary of our nation.

Our failure to continue to preserve and fight for our Common Laws has resulted in the dearth of information, access, and availability of our Common Laws. Have you tried searching lately? Why can't you find any books on it in any library? Or should we ask, what happened to all books on the Common Law?

Check this out. Go to your library, your Law library, any University library. Common Law books can be counted on one hand ......... if there are any books at all.

The Common Laws, recorded over centuries are at the heart of all the facts which serve as guideposts for us today. The Common Laws are based upon natural law, or God's law, and are inherent in the expression of free will being granted to man by his Creator. These are considered the eternal, immutable laws of good and evil; to which the creator himself in all his dispensations conforms, and which he enables human reason to discover, so far as they are necessary for the conduct of human actions. Such, among others are these principles: that we should live honestly; that we should hurt nobody, and should render to everyone its due.

The laws of such eternal justice are inseparably interwoven with the happiness in our guaranteed "life, liberty, and the pursuit of happiness". The pursuit of happiness is an individual pursuit. And such pursuit cannot be perplexed with a multitude of abstract rules and precepts, referring merely to the fitness or unfitness of things, as some have adjudged by legal acts, but are reduced to the rule of obedience to one paternal precept or foundation called ethics, or natural law. It is as simple as it is natural.

### *"That man should pursue his own happiness."*

The Common Law exists in man, is a part of his very being, is part of the understanding that he should "do unto others as he would have others do unto him". As long as his intent and motive to pursue his own happiness does not hurt another, he has the freedom and the free will to pursue his own happiness, and can do so; however, in doing so he takes on his own risk should he break the compact he has made with his creator.

The Common Laws which many of us today are quick to relegate to the annals of antiquity and replace with legislative acts, are the substantive laws of conscience from time immemorial. They are understood by all people and are as much a part of the checks and balances which protect our liberty and freedom as is the Republican form of government which gives us our sovereignty through reservation of our inalienable rights.

Now, bringing this up to today's understanding, we can look at the municipal application of the Common Laws and how the laws are meant to be carried out by the judicial powers within a state. Municipal Law is meant to be a rule of civil conduct prescribed by the state as a rule commanding what is right and what is wrong.

That is exactly an expression of the Common Laws. The Common Laws established such compact or agreement between the people and the municipality. REMEMBER: **We the People**, determine and promise what shall be done, before we are obliged to do it. That's why we vote. That's why we sign petitions and gather support. That's why we listen to what all of us have to say before we act. A compact is that promise proceeding from us. The language of the compact is I will or will not do this.

And conversely, municipal law is the rule to be followed and enforced. It cannot be legislated by legislature without our agreement. The language is simply I shall, or shall not do this.

**The specific difference between "will and shall" is clear: One is intent, and the other is performance.**

The Common Law preserves our rights to make and change agreements. We have the inalienable right to exercise our sovereign free will and to do so at the expense of the State or of any municipal laws. If any existing laws interfere with our freedoms we can declare such laws null and void, repugnant to the protections we enjoy in our original Constitution.

Knowing the Common Law: its early origins, the place of equity, the law of merchants, and by statute and Constitution, is only a computer window reflecting the reasons for the drafting of the early Common Law Documents preceding our original Constitution and surfacing in all of our State Constitutions.

They are not laws of the church or of canons often identified as Ecclesiastical laws. They are of the rights of sovereignty: that all men are to be considered equal, deserving of equal justice.

Their essence?

1. The fact that there has to be a DAMAGED PARTY in order to proceed under the Common Laws if a dispute arises;

2. The fact that the Common Laws cannot compel performance as in doing so individual rights are violated;

3. The fact that under Common Laws every contract has to be entered into knowingly, voluntarily, and intentionally by both parties, or the contract is as if it had not been entered into and is without substance. The substantive law applies.

4. The fact that the RIGHT OF TRIAL BY JURY shall be preserved in order to allow for decisions of average men considering facts to preclude decisions based upon legislative acts.

Yet even though the English Magna Carta of 1215 promoted the rights of individuals; in America, it was early documents such as the Northwest Ordinances (1787) which quickly followed our Declaration of Independence; and in turn gave us a Constitution **FOR** the United States of America, which subsequently required a similar Constitution be ratified in every Republic to give us a Constitution **OF** the United States of America.

We thus have two Constitutions:

*A Constitution,*
 *FOR:*
  *the United States of America*
*A Constitution,*
 *OF:*
  *the United States of America*

And knowing the difference between the terms "will" and "shall" is equally as important as knowing the difference between "for" and "of". Consider that each Constitution is subservient to the will of the people. Each Constitution is subservient consequently, unto its master.

**We the people** are the masters of the Common Laws having delegated them to our Constitutions – whether federal, national, or state – only limited powers.

Our "will" is a firm expression of our **intent** in our determination to retain our sovereign rights with our **mandatory enforcement** expressed by the term "shall".

*"This far shall thou*
*go and no farther."*

Section Two

# PRESERVING SOVEREIGNTY

## CAN YOU ANSWER THESE QUESTIONS?

## Questions: Preserving Sovereignty

(Answer yes or no: true or false.)

1. Because all men are created equal, you are sovereign.

2. Are you also sovereign because you are an American citizen?

3. The Bill of Rights guarantees your sovereignty.

4. Can you change the Constitution of the United States of America?

5. The United States of America is always the Nation.

6. The United States of America has one Constitution to be upheld and followed.

7. The Federal Papers were written before there could be a federal government.

8. In the eighteenth century, not all Americans of voting age could vote.

9. The federal government was delegated less than twenty-four powers.

10. Is the government today as oppressive as it was during the tea party revolution?

# ANSWERS: Preserving Sovereignty

1. TRUE  You are born free because of your creator.

2. YES  You are as you have Constitutional Rights.

3. TRUE  It places the federal government on notice that its own delegated rights are limited.

4. YES  By Amendment.

5. FALSE  It is a Nation internationally; as a federal government it is sometimes a nation.

6. FALSE  It has TWO– FOR the USA & OF the USA.

7. YES  As essays for ciizens to ratify the Constitution.

8. TRUE  Not until Article XIX, was ratified in 1920.

9. TRUE  18 are expressly delegated and stated in Article 1, Section 8. That's it!

10. YES  Today we have 40,000 oppresive bills passed. The Tea Party had 2 grievances: "no taxation; without representation".

## Section Two: PRESERVING SOVEREIGNTY

The intent of the Common Laws in America was to preserve the Sovereignty and rights of all citizens in the new Republic of America known as the United States of America. Such intent shocked the world historically, lawfully, and realistically as it challenged the heart of all previously known rights of heredity, nobility, and dominion over lands and property as well as people.

Sovereign, in early Webster 1828 dictionary definitions comes closest to that understood by our founding fathers:

"Supreme in power; possessing supreme dominion, as a sovereign prince. God is the sovereign ruler of the universe; also supreme; pertaining to the first magistrate of a nation; as sovereign authority; also a supreme lord or ruler; one who possesses the highest authority without control. Some earthly princes, kings, and emperors are sovereigns in their domains."

And sovereignty was defined then as "Supreme power; supremacy; the possession of the highest power, or of uncontrollable power. Absolute power belongs to God only."

It is no accident, then, that our founding fathers claimed their sovereignty came from God's law that all men are created equal.

Sovereignty had shifted to a right belonging to man, granted by the supreme ruler of the universe.

People were no longer to be considered vassals, subordinates, and slaves only to serve the pleasures of sovereign earthly rulers, who usually inherited their status or won it through force and continued to exercise it over all the people and lands under their dominion.

Our Nation was founded by people who claimed their freedom and sovereignty as a right derived from God. They wanted new lives in a new country; and although there was allegiance to the old country, the intense desire to be sovereign as man was their birthright.

The Great Seal for the federal government of the United States clearly affirms on its obverse Crest: a glory Orb, breaking through a cloud proper, surrounding an azure field bearing a constellation of thirteen stars argent. And on its reverse, the eye at the top of a pyramid is the Eye of Providence with the Latin motto Annuit Coeptis in the sky above – meaning *It (the eye of Providence) is favorable to our undertakings* or *He favors our undertakings*.) - Benjamin Franklin, John Adams, and Thomas Jefferson were given the task of creating the seal on July 4, 1776 and it was officially adopted on June 20, 1782.

**United States Seal:**

Sovereignty was an expression, then, of the natural, organic, God-given Right that man was created equal and such rights are natural as they are granted by the Supreme Authority: Providence. Thus, in 1772 at a Town Meeting in Boston, such rights although internationally a threat to the existing monarchy and ecclesiastical supremacy of many nations, were adopted and expanded to being;

COMMON LAW, SOVEREIGNTY, RESTORING THE TEA PARTY REPUBLIC

"the Natural Rights of the Colonists are these First, a Right to Life, Secondly to Liberty; thirdly to Property; together with the Right to support and defend them in the best manner they can – Those are evident Branches of, rather than deductions from the Duty of Self Preservation, commonly called the first Law of Nature –"

Sovereignty continues to explain such Natural Rights relating to Life, Liberty, and Property, and concludes the Rights of Colonists with the *force majeure* that:

"no men or body of men, consistently with their own rights as men and citizens or members of society, can for themselves give up, or take away from others."

"First, The first positive law of all Commonwealths or States, is the establishing the legislative power; as the first fundamental *natural* law also, which is to govern even the legislative power itself, is the preservation of the Society.

Secondly, The Legislative has no right to absolute arbitrary power over the lives and fortunes of the people...

Thirdly, The supreme power cannot Justly take from any man, any part of his property without his consent, in person or by his Representative."

These, then, were the Colonists' sovereign expression of the first principles of natural law and justice and the basic fundamental maxims of the Common Law: common sense and reason.

And again, the Natural Rights are expressed as Declarations by an act of the early American Continental Congress at New York, on October 19, 1765. This time, however, the rights are expanded as "humble opinions" respecting the most essential rights and liberties of the Colonists to protest taxes, duties, and to assert as a seventh right to establish sovereignty:

"That trial by jury is the inherent and invaluable right of every British subject in these colonies."

And as an eighth right in claiming sovereignty:

"That the late act of Parliament, entitled, "An act for granting and applying certain stamp duties, and other duties in the British colonies and plantations in America, etc." by imposing taxes on the inhabitants of these colonies, and the aid act, and several other acts by extending the jurisdiction of the courts of admiralty beyond its ancient limits, have a manifest tendency to subvert the rights and liberties of the colonies."

All such claim for personal Rights, as a natural course, are summarized with a firm reliance on the protection of Divine Providence and a pledge to each other of lives, fortunes, and sacred honor of the Colonists in their Declaration of Independence, as adopted in Congress on July 4, 1776 – now a matter of the historical records of *"The Federal and State Constitutions, Colonial Charters, and Other Organic Laws of the United States,"* compiled under an order of the United States Senate by Ben Perley Poore, Clerk of Printing Records. Washington: Government Printing Office, 1877.

Finally, to insure that there is no doubt, even in the new country, the United States of America, a Bill of Rights is agreed to and added as the first Ten Amendments to the Constitution when ratified on December 15, 1791.

Amendment IX expressly identifies the limitation of the new federal government and re-affirms sovereignty remains in the people.

"The enumeration in the Constitution, of certain rights, shall not be construed to deny or disparage others retained by the people."

And with even more specificity, Amendment X expressly identifies the limitations extending from the new federal government down through the individual States by reservation, and continues to re-affirm sovereignty remaining ultimately in the people.

"The powers not delegated to the United States by the Constitution, nor prohibited by it to the States, are reserved to the States respectively, or to the people.'

Should the States not claim sovereignty power over the federal government, when necessary; then the people are the ultimate power proving that they hold the *force majeure* and are the master over the servant State or federal government when not specifically delegated as a national government. The claiming of sovereignty meant freedom and liberty for all.

The Liberty Bell, to announce such ideas of sovereignty, could not ring until the people were prepared and ready to form a more perfect union and ratify a Constitution for and of the United States of America.

And such ideas of freedom and liberty had to be communicated to the common man; to all the Colonists. Thus, the Federalist Papers originally written under the name of Publius, were published and distributed to all of the thirteen proposed states.

## THE FEDERALIST PAPERS

Our Constitution was finished in September of 1787. But it had to be ratified by the individual states through popular conventions. The people of the states, rather than the state governments, had to approve the new document. Supporters of the Constitution had to appeal directly to the American people. It was not easy as the Colonists were reluctant to give more power to a central government controlled by an established political elite.

The Revolution promised power is in the local community and the hands of the common folk. Now the writers of the Constitution wanted to change all that. James Madison, Alexander Hamilton, and John Jay used the widespread and widely read newspapers of the day to distribute a series of short essays known as the Federalist Papers to influence America to accept and ratify a Constitution. The essays covered a broad range of topics, including presidential authority, taxation and representation, and the division of power between the national and state governments.

In the end, the newspaper plan worked. The Liberty Bell rang so long, it finally cracked. Americans were persuaded to support the Constitution, but the Liberty Bell could not ring in the Bill of Rights, which guaranteed the sought after freedom and individual liberty for all.

The Federalist Papers are now considered the first – and most important internationally – discussions of federal government. The Federalist Papers serve as a model of political reasoning, and so can readily be ascribed to the reason the Colonists were influenced and prepared to ratify a Constitution for the United States of America.

No other set of essays created such an international clamor for independence and a new kind of power in that eighteenth century. No man could believe or envision that Power actually emanates from the bottom up. Power is by the will of the people and is granted by Providence. That is what happened. The Natural law then, would soon be an Organic law in a written Constitution of the United States to protect the rights of all men created equal.

The sentiment swept the nation then and such is the sentiment which was later so historically and strongly expressed by President Lincoln in his Gettysburg Address on November 19, 1863.

*"That this nation, under God, shall have a new birth of freedom – that government of the people, by the people, for the people shall not perish from the earth."*

We are again at that same crossroad where sovereignty and liberty intersect. The basis for our Constitution is inherent in its Federalist Papers. But who knows of them? Our Constitution, after months of work, finished in September 1787 and is a document that cannot by any standard be ratified by the individual state unless their populations wants them to do so.

The Constitution FOR the United States of America is ordained and established in its Preamble by the People OF the United States.

Its Federalist Papers (number 39) established two things:

A country to be known as the
**United States of America (U.S.A.).**
A national government for that country to be known as the
**United States (US).**

All American citizens are Sovereign citizens OF the United States of America – the Country. They live under the Common Laws of the country (Nation) known as the United States of America (U.S.A.)

The United States, as such, is only a national government (US) representative of the union of all states, known as these United States (U.S.A.); and is not to be confused with the nation (country) known as the United States of America.

The only sovereignty delegated to the national government (US) is that of foreign commerce and treaties. It is this area where the States granted international powers to the federal government, albeit with the checks and balances accorded the separation of powers among the Executive, Legislative, and Judicial departments.

Section Three

# RESTORING THE TEA PARTY REPUBLIC

## CAN YOU ANSWER THESE QUESTIONS?

## Questions: Restoring the Tea Party Republic

(Answer yes or no: true or false.)

1. The Boston Tea Party was most about representation than the taxes.

2. The Boston Tea Party Indians detroyed the ships after the tea was dumped.

3. Do you have to obey a bill that is passed if it is repugnant to the Constitution?

4. Does the US actually own most of Alaska?

5. Washington DC is not a State.

6. Can the President make a Law for Congress?

7. Can a Lobbyist approach any Congressman?

8. Can campaign funds come from anyone?

9. Does Arizona, have the power to set, control and enforce immigration policies?

10. America is a Democracy.

# ANSWERS: Restoring the Tea Party Republic

1. TRUE.  Representation was most important.

2. FALSE  No ships were destroyed.

3. NO.  They are null and void & never existed.

4. YES.  Over 90% of Alaska is claimed by US.

5. TRUE.  Should it move it goes to Md & Va.

6. NO.  Only Congress has that power.

7. NO.  Only a Congressman within the district he votes in. Jurisdiction and venue control.

8. NO.  XIII Amendment. Congressmen lose citizenship for taking campaign funds from outside their district.

9. YES  All States are sovereign within their borders. X Amendment guarantees they have the right.

10. FALSE  America is a REPULIC growing out of a Democracy and thus is the model Republican form of government for the world.

# DÉJÀ VU

—A. Nicholaw

In 1773, in Philadelphia
Men bravely pledged
Their fortunes, lives and hearts
To form America: A Republic.
A great land, under God
Borne of Courage and faith.

In 1994, déjà vu,
Red Feather Fell.
The people heard not,
But the bell tolled deeply
Swiftly across a silenced country
Which could not weep

Knowing nothing of the sacrifices
Made by the common man
To keep and save
That once great Nation.

Asleep, Asleep!
In the comfort of complacency
Cowards, without consciousness
Continue to be ruled oppressively.

*Asleep, Asleep!*
*Not knowing that Concord shot*
*Heard 'round the World*
*Is again thunderously exploding*

*Proclaiming anew,*
*For all to hear*
*Red Feather's voice unfurled*
*As clarion of old:*
*Awake! Awake!*

*The sleeping giant rises up*
*Once more and tolls:*

> *"For Liberty*
> *And Freedom to all."*

## Section Three: RESTORING THE TEA PARTY REPUBLIC

**D**ÉJÀ VU: 1773 The English Parliament passed a tea act, taxing colonial merchants; and in doing so outraged the Colonists and united them in opposition. When the first small cargoes of tea consigned to Boston, New York, Philadelphia, and Charleston were not allowed to be unloaded, it was a shock to England. The tax was to be enforced and paid by midnight of December 16th. The reaction was swift and nonviolent. The English put up no resistance and the ships were not damaged.

The Colonists, disguised as Indians, boarded the tea ships in Boston the night of December 16, 1773 and dumped the cargoes into the water. The captain's log book, dated Thursday, December 16, 1773 stated:

> "Between six and seven o'clock this evening, came down to the wharf a body of about one thousand people, among them were a number dressed and whooping like Indians. They came on board the ship, and after warning myself and the customs-house officers to get out of the way, they undid the hatches and went down the hood, where was eighty whole, and thirty-four half chests of tea, which they hoisted upon deck, and cut the chests to pieces, hove the tea overboard, where it was damaged and lost."

The event was publicized as "the destruction of the tea" but was not recorded as the "Boston Tea Party" until the mid-30s, around 1834/5, when the new moniker was born, for opposing oppressive government control.

DÉJÀ VU: 2010. The tea party of 1773 united all of the Colonists under a moniker surviving today. Whether protesting as tea party members, as patriots, as occupiers, the opposition and clamor to correct abuses is louder than ever. It gives us our Republic and a Republican form of government.

The Republic is a renovation of the natural order of things, a system of principles as universal as truth and the existence of man, and combed moral with political happiness and national prosperity. It is the natural order to preserve liberty, property, and security as guaranteed rights of man. It extends the sovereignty of such rights into the political associations which comprise the nation and demands that such associations, whether individual, or as a body of men are only entitled to that authority which is expressly derived from the people.

What is called the Republic is not any particular form of government like democratic, aristocratic, or monarchy. It is wholly characteristic of the matter or object for which government ought to be instituted, and to which it is to be employed—RES-PUBLICA, the public affairs, or the public good; or, literally translated, the *public thing*.

It is a word of a good original, referring to what ought to be the character and business of government; and in this sense it is naturally opposed to the word monarchy which encompasses arbitrary power vested in an individual person, the exercise of which is the person, and not the **res-publica**.

The RES-PUBLICA, public thing has as its origin the Greek "Democracy"; however, there are many strong limitations in the Democratic form of government. It ultimately leads to the failure of a true Democracy in guaranteeing the innate rights of man.

The true distinction between a Republic and a Democracy is that in the Democracy the people meet and exercise the government in person. In a Republic, they assemble and administer it by their representatives. Democracy will, by necessity, be confined to a small spot. A Republic may be extended over a large region.

Democracy works well as a form of government where limited in scope of size and population it can conduct the RES-PUBLICA or the public business of a nation until, however, it becomes too extensive and populous. Democracy cannot work effectively as the separate parts soon become oppressive once becoming powerful. Space and size quickly destroy the effectiveness of Democracy. Ancient Greece discovered this quickly as power shifted from Athens, and the demand for centralized power in the government arose out of strength, not voice. Under a Republic, the public voice, as pronounced by the representatives of the people, is more consonant to the public good than if pronounced by the people themselves.

Our Tea-Party fought not so much for sovereignty, but for the public voice to be heard by abusive powers. Their voice, being unheard, soon results in a voice demanding to be heard. They wanted representation then, most of all. And when denied, the very voice which believed in natural law, gave birth to a new nation and a new form of government: the Republican Form.

This startled the world juxtaposing a new voice within a Democracy. A people's voice creating a Republican form of government: a government established and conducted for the interest of the public, as well individually as collectively. It did not connect with any particular form which the world understands. It defies being subservient to another power and declares itself sovereign by divine right and by voice. And that voice declares itself by representation.

Adding representation upon Democracy creates a system of government which embraces and brings together all the various interests and every extent of territory and population known. The Republican form of government immediately concentrates the knowledge necessary to the interests of the parts and of the whole. The whole is now the nation, the parts are states, the people are also parts of the whole, yet their collective voices, by representation, become the whole.

For once, government can be seen as the child of the voice of the people who created it. Every man is a proprietor in government, and has the duty to consider it a necessary part of his business to understand. The Republic concerns his interest, because it affects his property, his life, and his pursuit of happiness.

And these interests have costs which derive themselves from all men being created equal.

You can examine the cost and compare it with the individual or collective advantages. And your voice, alone must represent your examination before all others. With the advent of a Constitution enumerating what you grant, you do not have to adopt the slavish custom of following what in other governments are called leaders.

As Benjamin Franklin quickly noted when asked what kind of government is formed, he answered prophetically:

**"A Republic, if you can keep it."**

It is not easy to preserve and keep a Republic once it begins to fall away. The heart of the republic is the voice of the people and the voice of the people is expressed through its mandated representation.

How often have you heard representatives say, I voted for the "good of the country", or for the "good of the party", when the voice going unheard is the voice of representation which says...vote for the good of the **res-publica** within the district you represent?

Representation must represent only those constituents who exercised the sovereign right to put them in power and position to represent. Your Congress represents elected officials representative of a part of a whole. They are not the whole, nor can they represent the nation without consent from the majority of the other parts which form that whole. The whole is the nation; however, the voice of the nation is the people collectively expressing themselves through individual representatives.

A nation is not the body, the figure of which is to be represented by the human body; but is like a body contained within a circle, having a common center, in which every radius meets; and that center is formed by representation.

The representatives, too, represent themselves only as a part of their very constituency and are one voice within their collective membership when in Congress Assembled. There can be no vote taken by them for the "good of the country". As representatives sitting in the federal government, the "good of the country" only occurs concomitantly with the consent of the rest of the nation.

What is government but more than the management of the affairs of a Nation? It is not, and from its nature cannot be, the property of any particular man or family, but of the whole community, at whose expense it is supported; and through by force and contrivance it has been usurped into an inheritance, the usurpation cannot alter the right of thing.

Sovereignty, as a matter of right, appertains to the Nation only, and not any individual; and a Nation has at all times an inherent indefeasible right to abolish any form of government it finds inconvenient, and to establish such as accords with its interest, disposition and happiness. Every citizen is a member of the collective sovereignty; and as such, can acknowledge no personal subjection – his obedience can be only to the Common Laws.

As members of the national government, the good of the country is only that under powers given by citizens, and granted to the national government, such as the management of foreign affairs wherein the states waive all rights to make a treaty, enter into an alliance, receive a foreign ambassador, or deal in any way with a foreign government.

The balance of power, conversely, and ultimately, flows from the bottom up rather than from the internationally recognized top down. Such principles of Declaration are the truths to restore our Republic. They are reserved in the declarations made by the Tea Party forefathers. What have we learned?

That man has rights, – life, liberty, pursuit of happiness. This is the legacy left us. The ideal of individual liberty, that an individual has certain fundamental and inalienable rights which municipal, state or federal government can never override without permission.

Governments exist for the benefit of the governed to secure and protect those rights of man. Government is FOR the people.

And that these governments

### "derive their just powers from the consent of the governed."

Government is OF the people and BY their consent.

Whenever any government usurps power and becomes destructive of the rights of man, then it is the right of the people to overthrow that government, and when necessary to do so, it is also the right and duty of the people to establish a new government on whatever principles and in whatever form will insure to them life, liberty and the pursuit of happiness.

That under law and government, and in the protection of the rights of the people "all men are created equal" and must be allowed the fullest and freest exercise and development of their natural powers.

And to do so, our forefathers decreed: "there shall be freedom of speech, freedom of the press, freedom of peaceable assembly, freedom of petition. The homes of the people shall be secure against search, seizure, or intrusion, except by legal process. No person shall be twice put in jeopardy of life or limb for the same offense, nor shall any person be deprived of life, liberty, or property without due process of law."

Continuing, "no bill of attainder or *ex post facto* law shall be passed. The privilege of the writ of habeas corpus shall not be suspended, unless when in cases of rebellion or invasion the public safety may require it, but any one accused of crime shall enjoy the right to a speedy and public trial by an impartial jury of the State and district wherein the crime may have been committed. He shall not be arrested except by legal process; he shall be informed of the exact nature of the accusation; he shall be confronted by the witnesses against him, and shall not be compelled to testify against himself."

Wow! These decrees came down to us as part of the ancient laws in common. These ideals expressed were old, not new, at the time of the Tea Party and in 1776. The spirit that resisted the "tyranny of George III", that resisted taxation without representation in America, and stood for local self-government in domestic concerns, is the same spirit that opposes any oppression anywhere in the world.

The fundamental essential maxims and ideals of our liberties – the rights of self-government and self-taxation, of habeas corpus, trial by jury, and the right of citizens to hold their government responsible for conduct are ideals of a Republic as set forth in a Republican form of government.

Some of those who represent us now in Congress Assembled are ineligible to represent us and have lost their citizenship. Do you know the ORIGINAL THIRTEENTH AMENDMENT was passed in support of Article I, Section 9, of the United States Constitution?

*"No Title of Nobility shall be granted by the United States: And no Person holding any Office of Profit or Trust under them, shall, without the consent of Congress, accept of any present, Emolument, Office, or Title, of any kind whatever, from any King, Prince, or foreign State."*

Said original Amendment is a matter of record notwithstanding it being continuingly omitted in reproduction as it clearly provides the penalty for enforcement of Article 1, Section 9.

---

**The ORIGINAL THIRTEENTH AMENDMENT**
**Passed by Congress February 1, 1865**

*"If any citizen of the United States shall accept, claim, receive, or retain any title of nobility or honor, or shall, without the consent of Congress, accept and retain any present, pension, office, or emolument of any kind whatsoever, from any Emperor, King, Prince, or Foreign Power, such person shall cease to be a citizen of the United States, and shall be incapable of holding any office of trust or profit under them, or either of them."*

---

Is it any wonder, then, that the following two questions might just be answered with an emphatic: NO!

Can any lawyer or attorney taking oath to any Bar association which pledges itself to the Crown of England still be a citizen?

Can any Congressman, in the House or Senate, accepting financial support from corporations or lobbyists outside their constituency and venue still be a citizen?

Thus, it is time again to restore America to its rightful place in history as that nation which first introduced the Rights of Man as being the grantor of power and privileges to uphold and defend its rights.

To do this, the Republic needs the voice of the people once more. We need to speak again as in 1773 where the real intent of the Boston Tea Party was not to just dump tea in protest of taxation. It was to demand representation and voice. Again, today, **We the people,** need to speak.

It is our duty. Our rugged Constitution clearly gives us the Right to speak within our Bill of Rights with no less than six specifically identified amendments.

Article IX:
"The enumeration in the Constitution, of certain rights, shall not be construed to deny or disparage others retained by the people."

Article X:
"The powers not delegated to the United States by the Constitution, nor prohibited by it to the States, are reserved to the States respectively, or to the people."

Article XIV, Section 1.
"All persons born or naturalized in the United States, and subject to the jurisdiction thereof, are citizens of the United States and of the State wherein they reside. No State shall make or enforce any law which shall abridge the privileges or immunities of citizens of the United States."

Article XV, Section 1.
"The right of citizens of the United States to vote shall not be denied or abridged by the United States or by any State on account of race, color, or previous condition of servitude."

Article XIX, Section 1.
"The right of citizens of the United States to vote shall not be denied or abridged by the United States or by any State on account of sex."

XXVI, Section 1.
"The right of citizens of the United States, who are eighteen years of age or older, to vote shall not be denied or abridged by the United States or by any State on account of age."

Your voice is established by your Constitution as the *force-majeure*. And the method to speak in a Republican form of government is by vote. Today, at the latest count:

---

**DANGER**
Over 40,000 Bills Were Passed
During the Last Session
Of Congress

---

How has your voice been stilled? By omission? By being ignored? By misrepresentation? All are perpetrated fraud and constitutionally have no validity. Any bill which is repugnant to the Constitution of the United States is null and void and no man has to obey.

Here are three ways your voice has been stilled by Representatives. First, by their voting for the "good of the country"; Secondly, by their voting for the "good of the party"; and most dangerously, thirdly, by their voting for the "good of the lobbyists" engaged by private interests to secure favoritism.

It is impossible for your representative in the House to have read all of the 40,000 bills passed during the last session. It is impossible for the Republican form of government to exist when representation does not appear to allow the voice of man, the voice of the constituent to be heard. After all, the constituent is that person, that citizen, who gives up authority for one to act as a representative in municipal, State or in Congress Assembled.

It must be noted that this is a Constitutional Fact: no judicial decision, no jury decision, no appellate decision, no municipal, State, or federal decision in any court in the United States has the lawful, Common Law, Constitutional authority to overturn a plurality of citizen will.

*"Thy will shall be obeyed"*

Any intent to overturn any lawful vote may be done through the amendment process and the exercise of a new vote consisting of 75% approval from the original voting constituency.

**Let it be clear:** The security of a vote by res-publica is that vote prohibiting jurisdictional challenges and cannot be heard in any court, but only be amended by 75% of the same res-publica and constituents.

NO, NO!

> THE COUNTRY: has no CONGRESSIONAL CONSTITUENT voice.

> THE PARTY : has no CONGRESSIONAL CONSTITUENT voice.

> A LOBBYIST: has no CONGRESSIONAL CONSTITUENT voice.

Re-examine this ORIGINAL THIRTEENTH AMENDMENT as passed in support of Article I, Section 9, of the United States Constitution:

*"No Title of Nobility shall be granted by the United States: And no Person holding any Office of Profit or Trust under them, shall, without the consent of Congress, accept of any present, Emolument, Office, or Title, of any kind whatever, from any King, Prince, or foreign State."*

The original thirteenth amendment is a matter of record, nonetheless, it has been omitted in reproduction as it clearly provides the penalty for enforcing Article 1, Section 9, above.

The ORIGINAL THIRTEENTH AMENDMENT
Passed by Congress February 1, 1865

*"If any citizen of the United States shall accept, claim, receive, or retain any title of nobility or honor, or shall, without the consent of Congress, accept and retain any present, pension, office, or emolument of any kind whatsoever, from any Emperor, King, Prince, or Foreign Power, such person shall cease to be a citizen of the United States, and shall be incapable of holding any office of trust or profit under them, or either of them."*

## THE CONSTITUTIONAL VOICES

The only lawful constituent voices are those who can delegate representation in municipal, State or Congressional districts, and are limited to:

CITIZENS, who have been identified and are registered with district rights to vote for representation at municipal, State, or federal levels.

CORPORATIONS which have only recently been identified by the United States Supreme Court as being persons, who are now eligible under Article XIV, Section 1, and having corporate headquarters in a specific Congressional district. Said corporations may lobby (one vote) only in their district for representation at municipal, State, or federal levels.

We need now reformation of the process of creating and submitting bills for consideration and ratification. The following procedures are suggestive ballot measures to be sent via e-mail, blog, or what have you, to your representative or as a ballot measure for submission to voters on the next ballot to bring back the voice of America for the benefit of its people.

We are a Republic. Our Representatives shall say, "I voted as a representative of my constituency." Collectively, the constituencies are the Nation. Only they represent the country with their voice. A Congressman has only one voice – and that is as his own constituent from within his own district. Sovereignty is in the people.

## SOVEREIGNTY

The disquietude of the Mind
　　erupts with the magma of Truth
　　flowing overwhelmingly to submerge
　　the fiery falsity of control
　　over the Rights of Man.

Thus, in the flames of sovereignty,
a Republican form of government
　　of the people
　　by the people
　　for the people

In its relentless quest
　　for Life,
　　Liberty,
　　and the Pursuit of Happiness,

Is restored once more

In a tranquil sea of brotherhood.

— A. Nicholaw

Section Four

# HOW TO RESTORE THE REPUBLIC

Section Four: HOW TO RESTORE THE REPUBLIC

(in suggested ballot form)

1. Shall any bill presented for consideration in the House of Representatives as originated by a duly elected member to the House of Representatives be first ratified by not less than ten percent (10%) of the randomly selected voting constituents from within the State which is being represented?

2. Shall any elected member to the U.S. Congress be prohibited from making any appointments concerning submission of new or proposed legislation with any person, individual, corporation, entity, or vested interest group unless such person, individual, corporation, entity, or vested interest group be a voting member registered within his constituency?

3. Shall any person, individual, corporation, entity, or vested interest group desirous of having a bill submitted for consideration and presentation in the House of Representatives first submit such bill to its Representative for consideration by not less than ten percent (10%) of its randomly selected voting constituents, regardless of party affiliation?

4. Shall any bill, once approved by not less than ten percent (10%) of the representative's constituency, and to be submitted in the House of Representatives, be submitted first to not less than four other State Representatives in the House for review and ratification by ten percent (10%) of each of their randomly selected voting constituency before being submitted to the House of Representatives as a whole for ratification?

* * * * *

Such is the voice of the people restored. Given we can get to our Republican form of government, the clarity of law-making becomes obvious. Fewer bills to consider. No room for add-on pork-barrel programs which will quickly return to the State legislatures where they constitutionally belong, and most importantly: Maybe our representatives will spend more time at home to review legislation which their constituents want in insuring their sovereignty, their liberty, and their pursuit of happiness.

### Restoring the Republic Demands Action.

Are you ready to again claim your rights under the Common Laws?

Are you ready to again preserve your Sovereignty?

Are you ready now to demand your rights and end the powers of influence exerted upon your duly elected representatives?

Are you ready again to heed George Washington?

> *FAREWELL ADRESS: IF, in the opinion of the People, the distribution or modification of Constitutional powers be in any particular wrong, let it be corrected by an amendment in the way which the Constitution designates, but let there be no change by usurpation: for though this, in one instance, may be the instrument of good, it is the customary weapon by which free governments are destroyed.*
> *—George Washington*

Remember, always, your elected representatives work for you and should only represent your voice at all times. If they can't submit a bill without your consent, they may just come home to listen to what you need and want.

The Common Laws are about you once more; the sovereignty you justly claim is yours for the action; the restoring of the Republic is pending on your vote, your voice. Make it ring once more, but peacefully at the ballot box. Let them hear it loud and clear:

*"This far shall thou
        go and no farther."*

Section Five

# 101 QUESTIONS
# ABOUT THE COMMON LAW

## 1. What is the Common Law?

This is the first question which must be answered, and it is with a dictionary (Webster 1828) compiled during the Common Law period.

Our basic Common Law is what our forefather's called God's Law and it became the heart of law and rules of law which they wrote into the Articles of Confederation, the documents which preceded our Constitution, and finally, the Constitution of the United States.

> The nature & intention of a
>
> Constitution is to prevent
>
> governing by a party, by
>
> establishing a common
>
> that shall limit and control
>
> the power and impulse of
>
> party, and that says to all parties:

> **"This far shall thou**
> **go and no farther."**

## 2. What is the difference between Common Law and Equity Law?

The heart of Common Law is substance or Fact; the heart of Equity which came out of the Common Laws, is based in theories of liability and require some kind of damages – usually money. Common Law in practice is: "The impartial distribution of justice, or the doing that to another which the laws of God and man, and of reason, give him the right to claim."

Equity court corrects the operation of the literal text of the Law, and supplies its defects, by reasonable construction, and by rules of proceeding and deciding what is not admissible in a court of law.

The first Judicial Acts established a judicial system with the sole purpose of upholding our Constitution and basing decisions of the Common Laws which decided right from wrong.

## 3. What is Statutory Law?

It is the written law, which later became codified and called the Codes. Statutory Law originated in the unwritten Common Laws, but did not have their binding force in the principles of justice, nor of long use, nor the consent of the people or nation. Statutory Law has its binding force in the acts of legislative branch: the Congress.

## 4. What is Habeaus Corpus?

Coming from the Latin, the term simply means: "Having the Body." In the Common Law, it is a Writ presented to the marshal, sheriff, or court for delivering a person from false imprisonment.

"When we take from any man the exercise of hereditary power, we take away that which he never had the right to possess." No man has the right to falsely imprison another man.

"Our forefathers did not intend the Constitution should be interpreted by the judiciary." And the judiciary to issue arrest without due cause.

## 5. What is a Writ?

A Writ is that which is written. In the Common Laws, writs were prepared and submitted to the courts. Writs always originate with Planiffs and contain both a summons declaration of cause of action served upon defendant then recorded to bring complaints (cases) before the courts.

Without a Writ being served and proof that such service was made, the courts would not have jurisdiction and there could be no case.

## 6.   *What are the Common Law Procedures?*

There are seven basic Common Law Procedures:

1.   Jurisdiction of the Courts.

2.   Process to compel appearance of defendants.

3.   Pleadings.

4.   Trial.

5.   Judgment.

6.   Execution.

7.   Appellate Review.

All of the above seven Common Law Procedures are designed specifically to allow the courts to process the necessary complaint through the regular procedures to arrive at a remedy and redress which will satisfy the complaint and allow due process of law to occur.

### 7.   What is Jurisdiction under Common Law?

Jurisdiction depends upon authority over subject-matter and/or over the parties. Both subject and person must be had.

### 8.   How is jurisdiction obtained?

By personal service of summons, and sometimes on substituted service. Along with the summons is the written complaint. Both are needed to bring a defendant to court.

### 9.   What is a Common Law Filing?

It is called a Writ and is the original complaint which you want to serve upon someone. The filing can occur anytime after service.

### 10.   What is an Appearance?

The appearance of either a plaintiff or a defendant is simply any act or proceeding by which either places himself before the court as a party to the action. Appearance may be general or special.

### 11. What is a Common Law Pleading?

A pleading is the statement in a logical and legal form of the facts which constitute your Cause of Action and which you make against your defendant.

### 12. What is the object of Pleading?

Simply to let the defendants know your complaint, allegations, and statements – or specifically, to bring to issue what you both are arguing about and going to court about.

### 13. How Many Pleadings under Common Law?

Only ELEVEN.

### 14. Are they all pleaded the same way?

In procedure, YES; in substance, NO.

### 15. Is there an order to Pleading?

Yes. The order of Pleadings which you need to follow are to give organization and order in the trial. They are as follows:

a) Your Declaration (Complaint);

b) The Dilatory (delaying action) Plea of the Defendant to Defend or try to defeat your declaration.

c) The Demurrer of the Defendant to take exception to a point of law.

d) Your Demurrer, Replication to c).

e) The Demurrer or rejoinder of Defendant to d).

f) Your Demurrer or Surrejoinder to e).

g) The Demurrer or Rebutter of Defendant to f).

h) Your Demurrer or Surrebutter to g).

### 16. What is a Declaration?

A Declaration is the first step in Pleading. It is where you set forth and present your Cause of Action. It is a summary of the facts: date, time, place, where and when, and the manner in which you were injured and why you seek a remedy and relief.

> "Congress shall make no law........ abridging the freedom of speech or the right of the people to petition the Government for a redress of grievances."

## 17.   What are Common Law Causes of Action?

Causes of Action are substantive in nature. They contain the basic fact of your complaint.

*"The Constitution FOR the United States of America includes all the early Confederation constitutions, ordinances, and treaties."*
*"The Constitution FOR the United States of America is our county's Constitution: Of the People, By the People; For the People.'*

You have the Right, guaranteed by the Constitution. All Common Law is substantive.

## 18.   Are Causes of Action and Common Law Pleas different?

Yes. Pleas are answers to your declaration and are always founded on matter of fact collateral to your declaration. Pleas are classified as dilatory or peremptory – the one used merely to delay, the latter is an answer attacking the merit of the original complaint and cause of action.

## 19.   How are Dilatory Pleas classified?

a)   to the jurisdiction of the court;

b)   to suspend the Cause of Action;

c)   to abate (overthrow/destroy) the suit.

A plea to the jurisdiction is letting the court know that it does not have jurisdiction of the subject matter or of the parties standing before it and cannot hear the case or plea as it is barred from doing anything since it has no authority.

## 20. Are Pleas in Abatement and Pleas in Bar different?

YES. A Plea in Abatement is not directed to the merits of the controversy, as is a plea in Bar. A Plea in Abatement defeats the particular action but does not prevent the plaintiff from immediately bringing another action of the same cause. A Plea in Bar conclusively bars and defeats the right of Action.

## 21. What are Pleas in Bar?

They are those which go to the merits of the controversy and show some ground for barring or defeating the cause of action. They are also called peremptory Pleas, and are either made by way of traverse or by way of confession and avoidance.

A traverse is a denial of the whole or of a material part of the facts averred (positive statements of fact) by Plaintiff.

A Plea in confession and avoidance admits the facts to be true and introduces new matter to repel legal effect of such admission.

## 22. What is an Issue at Common Law?

An issue is a point at which you must go to trial. There are two kinds of issues: 1) in law and 2) in fact. An issue in law arises when the point in issue is a question of law. An issue in fact is when the point in issue is a question of fact.

A fundamental to the Common Laws are those which are orally handed down to us, introduced into our Constitution as Rights of Man and recorded as the Bill of Rights. Any law abrogating such law is repugnant. This, then, is a fundamental right.

"All laws which are repugnant to the Constitution are null and void. and no man has to obey them."

A further, and more contemporary example is:

Your vote cannot be abrogated by any judge. It is repugnant to Amendments XXIX, XXIV, and XXVI. It is a guaranteed Right.

"The claim and exercise of a Constitutional Right cannot be converted into a crime."

Your voting for a President who fraudulently has been elected cannot be construed to be a fact of collusion or intent to commit fraud once discovered. Your right to vote is protected. Your vote is null and void and the Common Law action can only render a verdict that will not hear any such complaint against you. The court has no jurisdiction over a subject that is null and void at the onset.

### 23.  *How are Issues Tried?*

Issues of law are always decided by the court, without a trial by jury, and after argument by counsel for both parties; however, under the Common Law and in all of the Republics, if a trial by jury is demanded, issues of law can be decided by a jury.

Issues of fact are always decided by the jury; however, where a jury trial is waived, the issue is decided by the court.

Under the Common Law, always reserve your most protected rights which are evidenced in our Amendments to the Constitution.

> "Amendment IV: The right of the people to be secure in their persons, houses, papers, and effects, against unreasonable searches and seizures, shall not be violated, and no Warrants shall issue, but upon probable cause, supported by Oath or affirmation, and particularly describing the place to be searched, and the persons or things to be seized."

> "Amendment V: No person shall be held to answer for a capital, or otherwise infamous crime, unless on a presentment or indictment of a Grand Jury; ... nor shall any person be subject for the same offence to be twice put in jeopardy of life or limb; nor shall be compelled in any criminal case to be a witness against himself, nor be derived of life, liberty, or property, without due process of law; nor shall private property be taken for public use, without just compensation."

Even though the courts will attempt to always ask you to waive your rights to a jury, you may do so simply by continuing to reserve them with a simple statement such as:

"All rights reserved under common law." The seventh Amendment, especially protects you.

"Amendment VII: In suits at common law, where the value in controversy shall exceed twenty dollars, the right of trial by jury shall be preserved, and no fact tried by a jury, shall be otherwise examined in any Court of the United States, than according to the rules of the common law."

## 24.   What is Evidence?

Evidence is that Proof arising from our own perceptions by the senses, or from the testimony of others, or from inductions of reasons. You can say it, smell it, feel it, see it, know it, but hearing it must be substantiated by personal affirmation or witness.

## 25.   How is Evidence Produced?

By your oral witness, or such witness by others; by the introduction of documents in open court as verified and signed by witness; by presentation of any matter believed to be material to the cause of action of subject to be verified.

## 26.   Who has to Prove the Evidence in a Trial?

You do — If you are the plaintiff. You have the initial burden of proof. You must prove to the court or the jury what you claim is the truth of the facts.

Once you have made your claim(s), the burden of proof shifts to the defendant. He must then prove you are wrong, deficient in pleading, or whatever. No matter, he must answer, or he has admitted to all your claims.

Once he defends, the burden again shifts to you until there are no other points of argument and both facts and law have been revealed.

The court never has the burden of proof to answer for the defendant(s); nor does any third party not identified specifically as a defendant.

Third parties can appear; however, they must first always have permission to do so in behalf of the plaintiff or of the defendant. That permission is granted by either the plaintiff or the court with the condition that if the plaintiff does not allow such joinder (bringing in another party) third parties are not admissible. They can only be appear as a witness.

The shifts in "burden of proof" therefore, must always be between the plaintiff and defendant and confined to the evidence as presented and not to new or extraneous matter.

> "In all criminal prosecution, the accused shall enjoy the right to a speedy and public trial, by an impartial jury of the State and district wherein the crime shall have been committed; which district shall have been previously ascertained by law and to be informed of the nature and cause of the accusation; to be confronted with the witnesses against him to have compulsory process for obtaining witnesses in his favor and to have the assistance of counsel for his defense."

## 27. Are there any Procedures to Producing Evidence?

YES. The steps to follow and the procedures you must follow in introducing evidence are:

The arguments of counsel.

The charge of the court to the jury instructing them as to the rules of law applicable to the issues and the facts which the evidence tends to prove.

The deliberation of the jury.

The verdict, which may be either general or special.

The judgment of the court.

The writ of execution.

More simply stated, these Common Law procedures can be restated as:

Cause of action; what law or rule covers the issue or fact you are presenting; what damages or injury you want reviewed; what other or related damage or injury suffered you want reviewed; what do you want court to decide or grant; and a final paper of judgment.

## 28. What is the Difference Between Interlocutory and Final Judgments?

An interlocutory judgment is one which defines the rights of the parties at an intermediate stage of the action or while the action is in process.

A final judgment is one which finally determines the rights of the parties and puts an end to the suit.*

*It must be noted, here, that Judgments include awards. The Common Law does not address awards (damages) but only addresses rights and injuries. Damages are pled in Equity law to remedy the right or injury.

## 29. What is a Civil Action?

Civil Actions are either legal or equitable. Legal Actions are divided into real, personal, and mixed. Real actions are those brought for the specific recovery of lands, tenements, or hereditaments –those things you inherit directly as property.

Personal actions are those brought for the specific recovery of goods and chattels, or for damages or other redress, for breach of contract, or other such injuries.

Mixed actions combine specific recovery of lands, tenements, or hereditaments & damages for injury sustained in respect of such property.

### 30. How many kinds of Actions are there under the Common Law?

Eleven kinds of Actions

### 31. What are the kinds of Actions of the Common Law?

1. Action of Account
2. Action of Covenant
3. Action of Debt
4. Action of Detinue
5. Action of Ejectment
6. Action of Indebitatus Assumpsit
7. Action of Replevin
8. Action of Special Assumpsit
9. Action of Trespass
10. Action of Trespass on the Case
11. Action of Trover

## 32. What are some Specific Kinds of Personal Actions?

Under the Common Law, actions ex contract
(out of contract or agreement) are:

    Account - Assumpit -

    Covenant- Debt -

    Indebitatus Assummpsit

Under the Common Law, actions ex delicto (without awareness, out of injury caused) are:

    Detinue - Ejectment -

    Replevin- Trespass –

    Trespass on the Case – Trover

## 33. Declarations have to have Formal Parts. What are they?

You must state the title of the court for jurisdiction;

You must state the venue (place) of the court;

You must summarize your action—such part is also known as the commencement;

You must make a statement of your cause of action which is the body of your case;

You must conclude your case.

Simply stated the formal parts are an outline of who does what, where did it happen, what happened, what is the problem, what do you want to solve (remedy) the problem.

## 34.   Why is the Declaration so Important?

First, a Declaration is your own personal oath that you specifically are telling the truth & giving such facts as necessary to support it.

Secondly, your Declaration is specific and you are saying the truth with particularity. What happened. How you are wronged.

## 35.   What is a Cause of Action?

The Real Complaint that you have. Why are you suing?

Is it a personal action out of contract – ex contract; or a wrong, injury you weren't expecting - ex delictu.

## 36.   Is there a General Rule identifying what You Need in Stating a good Cause of Action?

YES. The general points to be shown in a good Cause of Action are:

Your right to the complaint.
Defendant's wrongful act violating that right.
The injury or consequent damages to you.
Always keep in mind that the Common Law must be clearly and simply stated. Usually there is only one complaint identified. It is very easy to establish a right or wrong with only one issue (complaint) to consider and how little court time it would require to arrive at a decision. Consider also how little argument would need to be reviewed if the subject were singular rather than multiple with many allegations.

### 37. What are Allegations?

These are the specific facts which you allege, or state to be true. The defendant must be able to prove that your allegations are false, or have no bearing on what really happened.

Keep in mind it is important to state facts as the court and judges can address the law, but the jury is what ultimately protects you based upon the facts. Support your facts by affirmation if they are based upon observation or accident, or other occurrence not easily verifiable by quantity, product, or material evidence.

### 38. Are Allegations the Same as Causes of Action?

NO. Allegations are specific facts to prove your Cause of Action. The Cause of Action is your issue or major complaint. It often may not be based upon facts, but upon occurrences derived from facts.

> Ex. In Ejectment. The Cause of Action is wrongful eviction. The Allegation you make in ex contract is "My contract requires thirty days notice, which was not given"; and in ex delictu: "Defendant did not give sufficient notice, and I wasn't aware of any reason for ejectment at this time."

> Eviction is a fact, the wrongful action is the allegation.

### 39. Are there Different Allegations which must be Proven for the Different Causes of Action?

YES. There are some cross-overs, of course; however, your allegations are part of the procedures which must be followed. They are not the original substance, but the heart of the substance, the proof and support; thus, allegations are the Form of the Action used in procedure to support a cause of action.

## 40. What are the Essential Allegations which must be stated in a Cause of Action?

In ACCOUNT:

A statement of the facts showing the legal relation between you and defendant which gives rise to an accounting.

The refusal of defendant to account.

The damages or injury you sustain.

The Common Law does not require you to demand or give final notice to make an accounting. You have a Constitutional Right to seek an accounting and an opening of the books at any time you choose during normal hours of operation. Any refusal to set appointments or any ignoring of any request is deemed a refusal to make an accounting and actionable.

In COVENANT:

The execution of the covenant.

The Promise.

The Performance of Conditions Precedent.

The Breach. The Damages or injury.

The Common Law covenant is an agreement between two parties. The parts of the agreement are the promise to do something (terms) and how that promise is to be executed (terms). Any failure to perform by either party is actionable.

In DEBT:

A statement of the debt. What owed.

The Breach – Non-payment or return.

The Damages or injury.

The Common Law debt is a monetary or non-monetary thing. Simply stated it is an obligation to be fulfilled. Any law effected after the debt is incurred is "ex post facto" and cannot cancel the obligation. The statement (terms) are needed to be witnessed to avoid allegations creating doubt. Any failure to perform (by either party) is actionable.

In DETINUE:

Your right to certain goods and chattels of a certain value, the value of which is described specifically.

The unlawful detention or keeping of your goods or chattel.

The Damages or injury.

The Common Law detinue is to recover something – usually personal property – wrongfully taken by another. The right to recover the property is certain once proof property is yours and is actionable.

In EJECTMENT:

Your title to certain land or property.

The wrongful ouster or dispossession.

The Damages or injury.

The Common Law ejectment is recovery of that which, when proven you have title to (property), h seen wrongfully possessed or from which you have wrongfully been separated. The right to recover or repossess is actionable.

In DEBITATUS ASSUMPSIT (General)
The statement of the making of a contract and the terms of the promise on which the action is founded.

The consideration agreed to and given.

Your performance of all conditions precedent.

The Breach & The Damages or injury.

The Common Law debitatus assumpsit (general) is for breach of an express or implied promise, usually verbally made and not under seal, by which the defendant undertakes to do something or perform an action and does not do so. In general, it is usually breached when the implied promise to complete the obligation does not occur. The success here, is if the implied promise, when made, was witnessed. The extent of right or wrong is actionable.

In REPLEVIN:
Your title in certain goods at the commencement of the action.
The unlawful taking and detention ... or
The unlawful detention only.
The Demand and refusal in certain cases.
The Damages and injury.

The Common Law replevin always requires you make a demand to repossess property that is both wrongfully taken and wrongfully detained. It also works obversely, to repossess property rightfully taken but wrongfully detained. It is actionable.

In SPECIAL ASSUMPSIT:
The statement of the making of the contract and the terms of the promise on which the action is founded.
The consideration agreed upon.
Your performance of all conditions precedent.
The Breach.
The Damages and injury.

In Common Law, special assumpsit, the similarity to general assumpsit ends with the requirement that the specific terms of the agreement are clearly made and most often in writing and under seal. The specific terms and agreements, obligations of either party for performance are readily discernable and cannot rely on the "you said, I said; you promised, I promised" back and forth arguments. It is actionable.

In TREPASS:
For injuries to the Person.
the application of force by direct act of defendant.

the Damages or injury.

For injuries to real or personal property, or to relative rights.

your title or right.

the wrongful act of defendant causing direct injury.

the Damages or injury.

In Common Law, simply stated, an act committed against the person or property of another. Usually such acts concern wrongful entry on another's real property as distinguished from personal property –vandalism is a clear example. It is actionable.

In TRESPASS ON THE CASE

Your Right, Title, or Possession.

The Facts showing the existence of a legal duty on the part of the defendant.

A Wrongful Act by defendant in the Breach of this duty.

Damages or injury proximately caused by Act.

In Common Law, trespass on the case, concerns the right to recover damages that are not the immediate result of a wrongful act but rather a later consequence. Hence, the action today is under most of our tort laws such as negligence, nuisance. These actions are a result of failure or due to the original act. Vandalism is cause for repair which is the result (case) of the trespass – unlawful act against property. It is actionable.

In TROVER

Your possession or right of immediate possession of certain goods with:

Description of goods

Identifiable description of the property converted and your right thereto.

The value of the goods

Damages or injury.

In Common Law, Trover, is a serious offence, often criminal in nature as it is the conversion, by wrongful possession or disposition of another's property as if it were one's own. You cannot interfere with a another's right, whereby he is deprived of the use and possession of his property. The property must be certain, and the conversion must be willful in tort or criminal law. It is actionable.

### 41. What is an Example of a Legal Duty, the Breach of which Forms the Basis for a Cause of Action?

The relation of passenger & carrier, master & servant, or when defendant is in control of some dangerous machine or vicious animal.

In common law, the examples are clear. Defendant has primary obligation and duty to control the situation at all times.

### 42. Should Plaintiff Anticipate Defenses?

YES. In some jurisdictions the plaintiff must negative (deny) the possible existence of certain technical defenses such as contributory negligence, fellow-servant rule, and assumption of risk.

### 43. Why is a Demurer important?

If the allegations of the adverse party are legally insufficient upon their face (as stated) to sustain the cause of action sought to be enforced, or to constitute a defense, objection may and often must be by demurrer. It will lie for insufficiency of substance or form. It admits of the truth matters pled, but denies sufficiency in law.

A Demurrer can never be founded upon matter collateral to the pleading which it opposes, but must always arise on the face of the statement itself.

## 44.   What is a General Demurrer?

A General Demurrer is one which excepts to the sufficiency of the opposing pleading in general terms, without specifically disclosing the nature of the objection. It is sufficient where the objection is a matter of substance.

The Common Law requires addresses the substance only; however, no damages can be had when the law is not invoked. A general Demurrer cannot be used where the objection is a matter of law.

## 45.   What is a Special Demurrer?

A Special Demurrer takes exception to the sufficiency of the adverse pleading by showing specifically the particular grounds of such exception. A Special Demurrer can be a mixture of substance and/or law; however, it must specifically show which it rests upon.

## 46.   What do Demurrers Admit to?

Demurrers admit all matters of fact that are well pleaded. They do not admit matters of fact that are not well pleaded, nor do they admit allegations of conclusions of law or of fact.

The Common Law is the ultimate law of the land, and –

"By the law of the land is more clearly intended the general law, a law which hears before condemns; which proceeds upon inquiry and renders judgment only after trial."

Defendants, here, love to introduce other issues to avoid sufficiency. The Common Law does not allow this.

## 47. *What does the Court do with a Demurrer?*

It has to consider the whole record and give judgment for the party who appears to be entitled to it except:

On demurrer by Plaintiff to a Plea in Abatement where, on the whole record, the Plaintiff has not put his action on his right.
  Where there has been a discontinuance.
  Where questions of substantive right and not of form are to be considered.

The most dangerous thing to look for here is that the court will often (primarily indicative of prejudice) accept a demurrer as a matter of law when it cannot be sustained without first having specifically addressed the cause of action or complaint and found it to lack sufficiency or substance as a matter of law.

In Common Law, a judge cannot give judgment only on a demurrer. A demurrer, alone, is not enough for a judgment to be rendered if the defendant does not specifically answer the complaint or cause of action with the very law which it claims supports the demurrer.

An answer must be given or the court has no authority to dismiss or answer for the defendant.

## 48. *If you do not Demurrer, what must you do?*

You must plead, either by way of traverse or by way of confession and avoidance.

### 49.    *What is Traverse?*

In Common Law a traverse is a denial of an allegation of fact. You usually make a statement like:

"there is insufficient knowledge or information to form a belief concerning the facts."

You must state the facts.

### 50.    *Are there Different Kinds of Traverse?*

YES. In form. Traverse can be common which is an express denial of a particular allegation by defendant in the terms of the allegations, accompanied by a tender of issue or formal offer of the point denied for trial. The Special Traverse explains or sets forth grounds of the denial. It must consist of:

a)   the inducement; the verification.

The Special Traverse does not tender issue, it only denies.

### 51.    *If Special Traverse does not Tender Issue, Who Tenders the Issue?*

The other party.

## 52. What are Pleas in Confession and Avoidance?

These pleas admit the truth of the allegations and avoid their legal effect by alleging other and inconsistent facts. They do not tender issue, but conclude with a verification and prayer of judgment.

They are a) pleas in justification and excuse – admitting the facts alleged but show in effect there was no good cause of action;

And b) pleas in discharge – admitting the cause of action once existed but show it has been discharged by some matter subsequent either of law or fact.

## 53. What is a Dilatory Plea?

A plea which does not answer the general right of Plaintiff, either by denial or in confession and avoidance, but asserts matter tending to defeat the particular action by resisting the Plaintiff's right of recovery for damages or injury.

There are two Dilatory Pleas: a) Pleas to the Jurisdiction and Venue; and b) Pleas in Abatement.

Dilatory Pleas must be pleaded before any others.

## 54.   Is there an Order to Plea Dilatory Pleas?

YES.    First, Pleas to the Jurisdiction.
        Second, Pleas to the Abatement.

In Common Law a plea to the Jurisdiction or Venue is of first importance since the court has no authority to assume jurisdiction without
such jurisdiction being granted over person, or over subject matter.
    Such jurisdiction must exist separately over both parties: Plaintiff
and/or Defendant.

## 55.   What is a Plea in Abatement?

One that shows some ground for abating (terminating) or defeating
the particular suit without destroying the right of action itself.
    Pleas in abatement must be certain.

Ex. A landlord sues a tenant for failure and refusal to pay rent for six
months. The tenant refused to pay rent due to an act of God (tornado)
precluding occupancy. The landlord has to prove failure (refusal to
pay) precluded the act of God in order for the abatement clause to be
certain.

## 56. What are Pleas in Abatement?

Wrong venue or place of trial.

Personal disability of one of the parties.

The action is prematurely brought.

Another action is for the same cause is pending.

Nonjoinder or misjoinder of parties.


In Common Law, pleas in abatement, must be certain. Venue can be ascertained; disability can be identified, time frames can be identified, other actions are a matter of record, and nonjoinder or misjoinder requires only defendant show proof of permission to join having been made by plaintiff.

## 57. What are Nonjoinders or Misjoinders?

The wrongful joining or mistakenly joining of several causes of action or parties into a single suit.

In Common Law, any party seeking to be joined must first obtain permission from the Plaintiff, solely, or from both the plaintiff and the court. Anyone joining a suit can join in favor of either the plaintiff or defendant; however, joinder cannot be made without consent of the Plaintiff who can only rebut if a request for joinder is made.

## 58. What is a Writ of Error?

A process of a court of appellate or supervisory jurisdiction which issues the writ to an inferior court to remove the record for review for errors of fact or law in the proceedings as recorded.

In Common Law, a Writ of Error is also known as a Writ of Certiorari. It is clearly understood that any Writ – a demand or mandate by a plaintiff – is a Common Law Cause of Action and does not necessarily have to be issued solely as a process to remove the record for review. It is a review process, yet the Common Law reviews the facts to achieve remedy: a mandate to correct.

## 59. What is a Bill of Exceptions?

A statement of objections or exceptions taken by a party to the rulings of the court on points of law, signed by the judge who made the decision, and sealed with the seal of the court.

In Common Law, the Bill of Exceptions is an objection to points of law. Normally, this statement is to preserve the record for appeal; but knowing that a "trial by jury" is a common law right, and knowing that a jury can decide both the law and the facts, the appeal process is not always the next step. The court can simply be informed a trial by jury was demanded.

## 60. What is a Mistake?

In contract law, a mistake is where the parties did not mean the same thing, or while meaning the same thing, formed untrue conclusions as to the subject-matter of the agreement. When it has any effect at all, mistake renders a contract null and void.

Usually, mistake has multiple applications such as: a material fact directly related to the contract; a legal effect wherein one party did not know the legal ramifications of the contract; an equally, a mutual or unilateral mistake relating to some external circumstance.

In Common Law, mistake is an error and a writ of error issues from a higher court as the mistake application is pled.

## 61. *Is there a Remedy for a Mistake?*

YES. At Common Law the contract may be repudiated if it is executory; or, if executed in whole or in part, what has been paid under it may be recovered back. In Equity law a suit for specific performance may be resisted; or suit may be brought to declare the contract null and void; or, if the mistake is in the drawing up of the contract, suit may be brought to reform the instrument.

## 62. *What is a Representation?*

A statement made by one contracting party to the other, before or at the time of making the contract, in regard to some fact, circumstance, or state of facts pertinent to the contract, which influentially brought about the final agreement.

Representations may be oral or written; however, if not entered into the contract, the burden of proof that such representations were, in fact made, must be verified.

In the Common Law, oral affirmation is sufficient and such verification need only be witnessed if denied. If not, the oral affirmation is subject to jury determination by peers who know the veracity of the parties to the action.

### 63. What is a Fraud?

A false representation of a material fact, or the nondisclosure of a material fact under such circumstances that it amounts to a false representation made with knowledge of its falsity, in reckless disregard of whether it is true or false, with the intent that it be acted upon by the other party, and which if acted upon would cause injury.

In Common Law, any fraud is unacceptable. The truth is to be recognized and proposed. Fraud, specifically, is the deprivation of a right to property or to person. There is no specific action for fraud as all Common Law actions repudiate fraud as being actions against the rights of man which are natural rights protected by the common laws and protected by the organic laws inherent within our Constitution.

### 64. What is the remedy for Fraud?

In contract law you may affirm the contract and sue for damages for the deceit; rescind the contract, resist a suit in equity or specific performance; or sue in equity to have the contract avoided judicially.

In Common Law, fraud is actionable at all levels, across all inherent powers from executive (administrative), to executory (representative), to judicial (legal).

### 65. What is Duress?

The actual or threatened violence or imprisonment, by which a person is forced to enter into a contract. It renders the contract voidable at the option of the party who acted under duress.

### 66. Are there Different Kinds of Duress?

YES. Duress of the person is either duress of imprisonment, threatened with imprisonment or personal violence. Duress can be applied to personal property where it is threatened with unlawful destruction or detention.

### 67. What Kinds of Agreements are Illegal according to the Common Law?

Those involving the commission of a crime, and those involving the commission of a civil wrong, such as agreements in fraud of creditors or in connection with auction sales.

### 68. What is Undue Influence?

It is a species of fraud and may be said to consist of the taking unfair advantage of another in mind, in duress, in distress and will render any contract entered into null and void at the option of the injured party.

## 69. What is Admiralty Jurisdiction?

Admiralty jurisdiction depends entirely upon the locality, and includes navigable waters, natural and artificial, in their average state, but does not include wharves, piers, or bridges attached to the shore.

Tort must be consummated on navigable waters. If it commences upon the water but the injury itself was indicated on the shore, admiralty does not have jurisdiction, but where the primal cause of the injury is on land but the injury is consummated on the ship, admiralty has jurisdiction.

Detached piers, piles, or structures attached to the bottom, but surrounded by water, are within the jurisdiction.

Under the Common Laws, the Coast Guard is the only authorized jurisdictional officer of the court responsible for the collection of duties and imposts; hence, it is the senior legal officer over admiralty in debt obligations.

## 70. Are there other Kinds of Jurisdictions?

YES. Besides Admiralty, there is Maritime, Martial, Statutory, and Equity; however, today we are mostly concerned with what is known as Military (fringed flag representation) jurisdiction.

In Common Law (no fringed flag representation) there are only two kinds of Jurisdiction: Over Person (both Plaintiff or Defendant) and over Subject-Matter. The issue here is whether the granting of jurisdiction has been made to the court. Any challenge to the jurisdiction holds any proposed claim of action in abeyance until the jurisdiction has been settled to allow due process to proceed.

## 71. *What is the Object of Government?*

The true object of government is to secure the largest number of people the greatest degree of freedom and happiness.

The true object of government, under the Common Law is to secure the largest number of people the greatest degree of freedom and happiness according to their true representation and voice.

The Common Law always reminds the government that its object is to serve those who have created and delegated limited powers to it. The Common law reserves the balance of power to be equal over Administrative, Executive, and Judicial arms of government, reserving the true object of government to rest with those who granted the powers.

## 72. *What is the Object of All Laws?*

The sole legitimate end and object of all law is the security of men in the free enjoyment and development of their capacities for happiness.
The sole object of laws is: "do unto others as you would have them do unto you." And to secure life, liberty and the pursuit of happiness.

These are considered the moral and ethical laws as granted by God and the Right to Natural Law. They are the sovereign rights of men who are created equal.

### 73. What is the Difference between Federal Courts of Law and State Courts of Law?

Federal courts follow their own rules and may disregard the state practice with respect to the effect of appearances, the granting of continuances, the conduct of the trial, instructing the jury, allowing bills of exceptions, motions for new trial, motions in arrest of judgment, and other proceedings subsequent to the judgment.

In the Common Laws, the federal identification is not the Nation. The Nation is the United States of America which includes the states as unified into whole as a nation.

The federal courts, thereupon, do not represent the individual states and may follow separate rules and procedures with respect to proceedings in law.

The state courts must follow the nationally recognized statutes and codes as well as those within their jurisdictions (their separate legislated actions) and in agreement with differing state legislated actions provided said legislated actions are Constitutionally valid.

## 74. What is Process?

Process issues upon filing. It is the basic summons you send to a defendant. Currently service of process must be strictly followed: "that service of subpoenas shall be by delivery of a copy thereof by the officer serving the same, to the dwelling-house or usual place of abode of each defendant, with some adult person who is a member or resident in the family." A return is expected or an affidavit accordingly to show such service was accomplished.

Besides jurisdiction, Process must include Complaint as a Cause of Action, allegations- the thing to be or not to be- and the damages sought or injury to be remedied.

## 75. What Are the Rules of Governing Abatement?

Every defense heretofore presentable by plea in bar or abatement shall be made in the answer and may be separately heard and disposed of before the trial of the principal case in the discretion of the court. If the defendant moves to dismiss the bill (filing) or any part thereof, the motion may be set down for hearing by either party upon notice, and, if it be denied, answer shall be filed.

Again, in the Common Law, should any defense pled in Abatement be denied, an answer to the cause of action must be made. Answers to allegations alone, cannot deny the need for lawful answer to the complaint. Without said lawful answer, no judgment can be rendered by the court and under the common law a jury trial is warranted.

### 76. *What are the Rules of Law?*

There are two basic classes:

Rules of Substantive Law relating to the means of RIGHTS and OBLIGATIONS OF MEN.

"Substantive Law consists of the Common Law of rights and remedies."

Rules of Adjective Law relating to the means of enforcing RIGHTS and OBLIGATIONS OF MEN.

"Adjective Law consists of the Common Law of theories of liability."

> "The right of the people to be secure
> in their persons, houses, papers, and
> effects against unreasonable searches
> seizures, shall not be violated, and no
> warrants shall issue but upon probable
> cause, supported by Oath or Affirmation."

### 77. *What is Evidence?*

All the means by which any alleged matter of fact, the truth of which is submitted to investigation, is established or disproved; it includes whatever is legally submitted to a court or jury, whether it be by matter of record or writing, or by the testimony of witnesses, in order to enable the jury to decided upon the question in dispute.

## 78.  What is Proof?

The conviction or persuasion of the mind of a judge or jury, by the exhibition of evidence, of the reality of the facts you have alleged to be true. The reality that the opposite position of a fact of truth—as presented—cannot be sustained, is also proof and evidentiary.

Evidence is the medium by which the truth is established, while proof is the effect of such evidence. Proof can only be established by means of the evidence, but evidence does not always establish proof.

## 79.  What is Judicial Notice?

There are certain facts of which the court will not require evidence because the facts are so well known, so easily ascertainable, or so related to the official character of the court, there is no need to present evidence to support the facts. Judicial notice of the laws as it pertains to known facts is, however, important to be made.

In the Common Law, there is only precedence currently common which can be noticed as the Common Law is oral and always operates under those laws which are established and accepted by tradition, custom, and usage.

Under the Common Laws, judicial notice seems superfluous as facts are the ultimate decision of the jury and peers, not the court, and such facts are material and relevant even if deemed redundant, to be presented to a jury of peers.

### 80. What is the Difference Between Questions of Law and Questions of Fact?

Wherever the thing to be determined involves the application of some principle of the Statute or Common Law, it is a question of law.

The question of the existence or nonexistence of a CERTAIN STATE OF THINGS or CONDITION is a question of fact.

### 81. Is The Constitution the Supreme Law of the Land?

YES. The Constitution FOR The United States of America is the Supreme Law of the Land. The Constitution herein is representative of the whole of the states as united with such laws and powers as are delegated in part or wholly by each or all of the united States. Here, then, the exclusively delegated powers in international application of law allows the Constitution to be the Supreme Law of the Land.

NO. The Constitution OF The United States of America is not the Supreme Law of the Land. The Constitution herein is representative of the parts of the separate states with such laws and powers as reserved under the Constitutional Amendments IX and X. which include all sovereign rights not enumerated within the Constitution.

Under the Common Laws, such sovereign rights are identified as the Rights of Man and are:
God's Law, deemed Providence.
Natural Law, as granted by God.
Organic Law as vested in our Constitution.

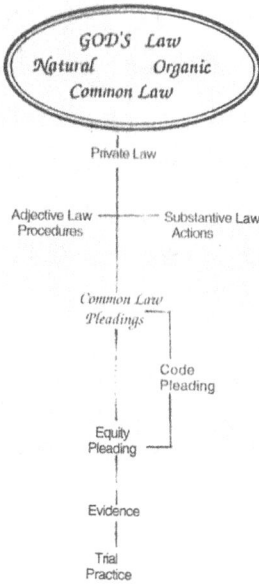

The Common Laws are the unwritten laws passed down; and Adjective Laws are procedures while Substantive Laws are actions which under the Common Laws become Pleadings for statutory, code, or equity pleadings in courts of law. Equity pleading is process, and evidence, and trial practice are procedures and process.

## 82. Where is the Enforcement Power for the Supreme Law of the Land?

Identification specifically for the enforcement power is by name only. The true enforcement power is invested in the people of the United States of America. *We the people* are the Supreme Law of the Land for the United States of America through our voice and vote which delegated to and authorized representation for the Republic of the United States of America. Only the enforcement power has the power to dissolve what it has created, and it can do so by amendment.

### 83. How can the Common Law and the Constitution be both the Law of the Land at the same time?

The Constitution OF the United States of America is only the law of the land as a national government, not as that of the NATION.

The Constitution FOR the United States of America is the law of the nation, not the national government.

The Common Law is the expression of the nation as a whole: It is the expression of the Will of the People, in Congress Assembled, and is the real law of the land.

### 84. In Simple Terms, What's the Bottom Line of the Common Law where anyone can say is the Heart of the Common Law?

No other way to say it:

"DO UNTO OTHERS AS YOU WOULD HAVE THEM DO UNTO YOU"

### 85. What is the Difference Between Remedy and Relief?

The Common Law decides between Right and Wrong. The Remedy for an Action is a satisfaction for being either right or wrong.

A Relief for an Action is an award of Equity as damages for injury which satisfies the prevailing party for being right.

### 86.  What is Injunctive Relief?

The value for the complainant filing an injunctive relief action must show that he has no plain, adequate and complete remedy at law, and that an irreparable injury will result unless the relief is granted.

### 87.  Is there a Difference between Common Law and Equity Mortgages?

YES. At Common Law a mortgage conveys the entire legal estate, subject to be defeated by a strict performance of the conditions. This is a very real difference. The key word is convey. The land, by deed, must be transferred.

In Equity Law a mortgage is regarded primarily as a security for a debt, the mortgage having but a lien on the land to secure payment. This is why currently equity mortgages were shopped around and it cannot be proven that the land has, in effect, ever been conveyed.

### 88.  What is Equity?

Equity is a system of jurisprudence which affords a remedy where there is no plain, complete, and adequate remedy at Common Law.

Equity will not suffer a wrong to be without a remedy – whenever a legal right is infringed, equity will provide a remedy IF there is none through the Common Law. Equity cannot preclude Common Law pleadings.

### 89. *How do you Define the Truth?*

By Declaration. Any declaration is presumed under the Law to be true. The Burden of Proof is on the Defendant to disprove the declarations. Some such statements regarding Truth are:

"The truth is conformity to fact
or reality; exact accordance with
that which is, or has been, or shall be."

"My mouth shall speak the truth.
Snctify them through thy truth.
Thy Word is truth."

"Witnesses as sworn to tell the truth
the whole truth, and nothing but
the truth."

### 90. *Are Allegations and Accusations the Same?*

NO. Allegations are assertions of Fact where Accusations are charges against a person or corporation. Broadly, accusations may be made by complaint, indictment, presentment, information, or inquest.

A complaint is an accusation by a private person, under oath and is generally allowed in the case of misdemeanors.

An indictment is a written accusation, proffered to the grand jury by the prosecuting officer, and found by them to be well founded.

A presentment differs from an indictment only in that it is an accusation made by the grand jury of their own motion, and upon their own knowledge or information.

## 91.  What does Particularity Mean?

Exactly. A name spelled wrong is not Particular and is cause for failing to be exact.

In Common Law, facts must be stated with particularity and when made orally under oath are assumed to be true; however, when disputed, must be verified with specificity of evidence whether by further witness, or by direct or material evidence.

## 92.  Does Property have to be Described with Particularity?

When property is the subject of the Complaint, whether real or personal, it should be described with sufficient particularity so as to identify it. Names, dates, times, places must be accurately given so as to be readily verifiable.

In those cases in which a value is material, as in case of larceny, the exact value must also be stated so as to be readily verifiable.

Expert witnesses may be less than reliable, therefore, their credibility must be established with particularity.

### 93. What is the Difference between Real and Personal Property?

Essentially, Real Property is anything which is so connected to land that it cannot be removed without permanent injury thereto. Personal property is simply all movable property.

A gray area is hereditaments wherein in the Common Law of Seisin requires proof of title and contract laws governing bonds secured by liens on property seized by eminent domain process are considered "real property" in effect as the holder of the bond is, in effect, owner of the property not truly surrendered until paid for.

> "As Property, honestly obtained is best secured by an Equality of Rights, so, ill-gotten property Depends for protection on a Monopoly of Rights."

## 94.  *What is a Fact?*

A fact may be anything of which a past or present existence may be asserted or stated and, as such, be verified. Specifically defined as:

Ordinary facts are also known as ultimate facts which, under the Common Law or substantive law attach legal consequences.

Evidentiary facts also exist yet you must understand that Substantive Law does not attach any legal consequences to evidentiary facts.

They can, if stated in sufficient detail give credibility to ultimate facts, but only by inference.
     You need to know that in pleading, do so with ultimate facts such as ordinary or operative fact which have legal consequences.

You need to know that in pleading with evidentiary facts you may be pleading and making conclusions of law which are unverified and dependent upon the court to draw the conclusions necessary to arrive at the truth.

The Common Laws require all evidentiary law to be substantively supported by separate witness or documentary material evidence as witnessed.

## 95. *How do you Create a good Cause of Action?*

Causes of Action depend upon and are prescribed by Substantive Law applicable to SPECIFIC FACTS of the Particular Case.

In Common Law they are identified in these 101 Questions About the Common Law.

## 96. *How do you Create a good Form of Action?*

Form of Action is dependent upon Theories of Liability. You must state the Combination of fact or Event which involves your selection of allegations as required by the Substantive (Common Law) Pleading.

Your allegations are essential to the statement of the specific Cause of Action which you are stating.

Try always, under the Common Law pleadings to keep allegations directly related to your cause of action and not introduce any subject-matter which will stray.

## 97. What are the Specific Differences between Cause of Action and Form of Action?

In general summary, a Cause of Action allows for incidental differences in Procedure and creates precedent Writs whereas –

A Form of Action keynotes the theories of liability and the procedures which are needed to support and prove the original Cause of Action and Complaint.

> "A complaint may not be dismissed on motion if it states some sort of claim, baseless though it may prove to be and inartistically as the complaint may be drawn. This is particularly true where the Plaintiff is not represented by counsel."

## 98. Are a Declaration & Cause of Action the Same?

NO. Your Declaration is, in fact, a summary statement of all he material facts in the Cause of Action, and consists of:

Title of Court (Municipl, Superior, District).
The Venue.
The Commencement (How the Case came about).
The Statement of the Cause of Action & The Conclusions.

## 99. What is the Most Important Thing for a Plaintiff to Remember?

You must state in the Declaration distinctly and with certainty every fact that is essential to:

PLAINTIFF'S RIGHT.

DEFENDANTS WRONGFUL ACT VIOLATING THAT RIGHT.

THE CONSEQUENT DAMAGES OR INJURY.

## 100. Where are there Courts Practicing Common Law?

There are no Common Law courts today. There are cases being submitted "at law" but the present system does not provide a true common law court which will accept common law pleadings and follow the rules of the Common Law.

Until juries are apprised and trained in the rules of the Common Law; until counsel with titles are barred from appearing as counsel at Common Law; until the judiciary is apprised and trained in the rules of the Common Law, you do not have any today.

### 101. If there are No Common Law Courts, How do we get the Common Law back into our Court System?

The Common Law as identified in every Republic's First Legislative Acts shows how to convene a Common Law court with a Common Law jury.

The Common Law rules are identified in every Sheriff's original book of instructions.

The Common Law is the Rule of Decision today wherever there is a conflict between the federal laws, the state laws and the Constitutional laws not delegated or enumerated. It is only for you to remember that the First legislative Acts of your Republic should show how to establish a Common Law Court. Should they not, your Sheriff should check the original records.

You will need our Original Flag, without a fringe denoting admiralty, a set of records for a cout recorder, and a bible to take an oath on. No other frills. A place for a judge, a place for a jury, if required. You do not need the bar which in reality stood for barrister –a lawyer and servant of the Crown of England.

All may exist in archives, but are records that reflect the truth of custom and precedence.
This is the COMMON LAW:

*"Law, in its regular course of
administration through courts
of justice is Due Process of Law."*

And LIBERTY IS JUSTICE FOR ALL.

And **We the people**, are still the final decision makers in all cases where a trial by jury is requested for. We are a Nation of Laws and must protect them vigorously and refuse to accept any legal actions which are designed to rob us of our sovereignty, our freedom and Liberty.

Our courts can only go so far when we lose our voice. To Restore our Republic we must first restore our Constitution, our Balance of Powers between Administrative, Legislative, and Executive, branches of government. Our voice needs to be heard once more.

Our forefathers repeatedly told its Congress:
  "That a Constitution was created to serve a Republican form of government, and that that very Republican form of governement only gave its federal government some eighteen delegated and limited powers." The truth is plain and simple!

*"This far shall thou
go and no farther."*

FIRST CHARGE TO THE JURY
   Chief Justice Jay

*"It may not be amiss, here, gentlemen, to remind you of the good old rule, that on questions of fact, it is the province of the jury; on questions of law, it is the province of the court, to decide.*

*But it must be observed that by the same law, which recognizes this reasonable distribution of jurisdiction, you have, nevertheless, a right to take upon yourselves to JUDGE OF BOTH, and to determine THE LAW AS WELL AS THE FACT in controversy—even that the court are the best judges of law.*

*But still both objects (law and fact) are lawfully within your power of decision."*

## PATRIOT

Red:
> *Deep, deep*
> *Passion pulses its blood*
> *Through bulging veins of life:*
> *Unending thirst*
> *That men be free.*

White:
> *Pulsing, pulsing*
> *Its wave rises*
> *Mountainous crest of sea:*
> *Broad ..... strong .....*
> *Of God .... Country .....*
> *Man.*
> *Listen! A Nation's Soul awakes!*
> *Its rhythm beats*

Blue:
> *Universal tears of*
> *Love,*
> *Harmony,*
> *Gone astray.*

*Break, break, 'O Waves*
*Scatter your force of freedom*
*Refresh! Bathe!*
*Drown the thirst*
*Drink deep, Deep!*
*Your measured cup spills racingly*

*Drink quickly.*
*The Passion*
*The Crest*
*Is soon gone.*

*— A. Nicholaw*

www.ingramcontent.com/pod-product-compliance
Lightning Source LLC
Chambersburg PA
CBHW072314290526
45794CB00002B/659